ENGLAND

ENGLAND

ENGLAND

D1120150

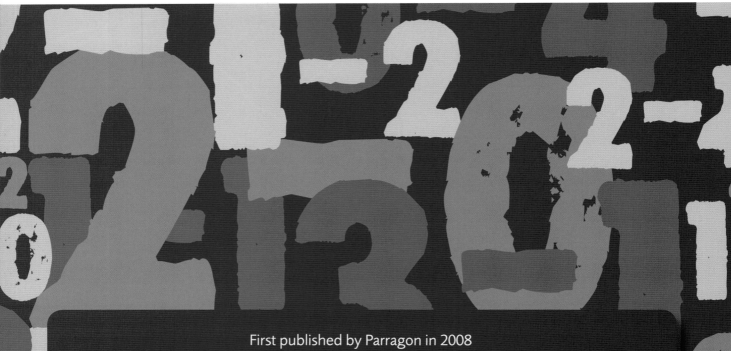

First published by Parragon in 2008
Parragon
Queen Street House
4 Queen Street
Bath BA1 1HE, UK

TheFA.com

All information correct at time of creation, March 2008

ISBN 978-1-4075-3233-2

Printed in China

Contents

Section 1 – Profiles   7
Stats and facts about the stars of the England team.

Section 2 – Positions   25
Great trivia, debut info and position techniques.

Section 3 – Activities   37
Top quizzes and puzzles to test your footy knowledge.

Section 4 – Great Games   53
From clashes in the 1966 World Cup, to struggles with Cameroon and Argentina, read up on a selection of England's memorable games.

Section 5 – England Legends   65
A selection of past England players who truly deserve the title 'legend'.

Section 6 – Tournaments & Rivals   77

England and the World Cup   78
Goals, glory and all those nerve-racking penalty shoot-outs.

England and the European Championship   82
England's highlights in the quest to find Europe's best footballing country.

England's Rivals   84
England's healthy rivalry with certain world-class teams. Here we look at four of the best.

ENGLAND

How much do you know about your favourite players? Read this section to get the low-down on England's top football stars of the moment.

Team Profile

The England team line up for their first game of 2008 against Switzerland.

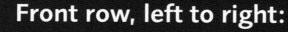

ENGLAND v SWITZERLAND
WEDS 6th FEBRU...

Nationwide
THE ENGLAND TEAM SPONSOR

Front row, left to right:

Ashley Cole, Steven Gerrard, Wayne Rooney, David Bentley and Joe Cole

Team Profile

Back row, left to right:

David James, Matthew Upson, Rio Ferdinand, Wes Brown, Gareth Barry and Jermaine Jenas

Player Profiles

Paul Robinson

Born: 15.10.79, Beverley, Yorkshire
Height: 6ft 4in
Club side: Tottenham Hotspur
Previous Club: Leeds United
England Debut: 12.02.03, against Australia

Despite being a goalkeeper, Paul has scored two goals: a header, when he played for Leeds, and a long-range free-kick from inside his own half for Spurs. 'Robbo' is one of the most reliable goalkeepers in the Premiership. He uses his physical presence to claim crosses and create a barrier between the defenders and the goal. Paul's shot-stopping skills and ability to command the goal area have helped the Spurs star confirm his position as one of England's best goalies.

Scott Carson

Born: 03.09.85, Whitehaven, Cumbria
Height: 6ft 3in
Club side: Aston Villa (on loan from Liverpool)
Previous Clubs: Charlton Athletic (on loan), Sheffield Wednesday (on loan), Leeds United
England Debut: 16.11.07, against Austria

Scott once held the record for most appearances for the England Under-21s side, with 29 appearances in total. Scott's younger brother, Grant Carson, is also a goalkeeper, for Carlisle United.

ENGL

David James

Born: 01.08.70, Welwyn Garden City, Herts
Height: 6ft 5in
Club side: Portsmouth
Previous Clubs: Manchester City, West Ham, Aston Villa, Liverpool, Watford
England Debut: 29.03.97, against Mexico

David played in all of England's matches during Euro 2004. He is the first Portsmouth player to play for the England team since Mark Hateley in 1984.

Chris Kirkland

Born: 02.05.81, Leicester
Height: 6ft 5in
Club side: Wigan Athletic
Previous Clubs: West Bromwich Albion (on loan), Liverpool, Coventry City
England Debut: 16.08.06, against Greece

A consistent keeper with excellent distribution, Chris Kirkland is one of several goalkeepers vying for the England number one jersey. A good organiser capable of pulling off spectacular saves, the Wigan stopper will be aiming to add to his one cap tally in the next few seasons.

Player Profiles

Nicky Shorey

Born: 19.02.81, Romford, London
Height: 5ft 9in
Club side: Reading
Previous Club: Leyton Orient
England Debut: 01.06.07, against Brazil

Nicky started his career as an apprentice at League Two Leyton Orient in 1998. The left-back quickly made his mark in 2006/2007 playing for Reading, displaying spectacular deliveries from both set pieces and causing havoc among the opposition with his open play.

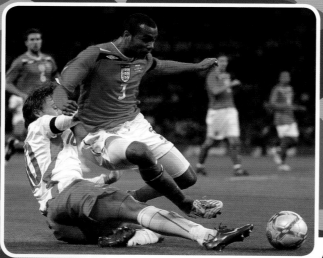

Ashley Cole

Born: 20.12.80, Stepney, London
Height: 5ft 8in
Club side: Chelsea
Previous Clubs: Crystal Palace (on loan), Arsenal
England Debut: 28.03.01, against Albania

Ashley started his career as a striker, before Arsenal manager, Arsene Wenger, transformed him into an attacking left-back. Ashley has earned a reputation as one of the finest left-backs in the world due to his tight defensive displays, pace and creativity going forward. The Chelsea man gives England a natural balance down the left, helping the team attack and also tracking back at speed to stop the opposition scoring.

Phil Neville

Born: 21.01.77, Bury, Manchester
Height: 5ft 11in
Club side: Everton
Previous Club: Manchester United
England Debut: 23.05.96, against China

Phil used to play cricket for England at youth level. Now a footballer, Phil can play on the right or left, and also in midfield. His versatility is great for England.

Wayne Bridge

Born: 05.08.80, Southampton
Height: 5ft 10in
Club side: Chelsea
Previous Club: Fulham (on loan), Southampton
England Debut: 13.02.02, against Holland

Wayne played in The FA Cup Final in 2003. 'Bridgey' is an excellent defender and battles Ashley Cole in both club and country for a starting spot.

13

Player Profiles

Ledley King

Born: 12.10.80, Bow, London
Height: 6ft 2in
Club side: Tottenham Hotspur
Previous Club: None
England Debut: 27.03.02, against Italy

Ledley holds the record for the fastest goal ever scored in a Premier League match after he scored after just ten seconds against Bradford City in 2000. This Spurs stopper provides excellent cover for Rio and 'JT', and always performs well when called upon by his country. Using his pace and strength to dominate the heart of Tottenham's defence, he is awesome in the air, winning nearly every header he jumps for. He can also play in the midfield holding role, too.

Rio Ferdinand

Born: 07.11.78, Peckham, London
Height: 6ft 2in
Club side: Manchester United
Previous Clubs: Leeds United, AFC Bournemouth (on loan), West Ham
England Debut: 15.11.97, against Cameroon

Rio is one of the calmest and most naturally gifted defenders in world football. His composure on the ball and ability to read the game like a book means he's rarely caught out of position and is able to pass the ball wherever he wants. Rio and fellow defender, John Terry, make England very solid at the back. Rio's brother, Anton, plays for West Ham and is also a central defender.

14

Player Profiles

Steven Gerrard

Born: 30.05.80, Whiston, Merseyside
Height: 6ft
Club side: Liverpool
Previous Club: None
England Debut: 31.05.00, against Ukraine

Steven was named as Steve McClaren's England vice-captain in August 2006. 'Stevie G' is one of England's best players. His speed, strength and skill on the ball make him one of the most talented midfielders around. The Liverpool captain often scores spectacular long-range goals, as well as creating loads of chances for his England team-mates with his accurate passing and great vision.

Frank Lampard

Born: 20.06.78, Romford, Essex
Height: 6ft
Club side: Chelsea
Previous Clubs: Swansea City (on loan), West Ham
England Debut: 10.10.99, against Belgium

Chelsea star 'Lamps' has excellent energy levels and awesome passing skills. Frank offers a great goalscoring threat for England, as his clever forward runs and ability to smash the ball into the net from any distance or angle make him one of the Three Lions' key players. Frank's dad, Frank Lampard Snr, played for West Ham and also earned two caps for England.

Player Profiles

Owen Hargreaves

Born: 20.01.81, Calgary, Canada
Height: 5ft 11in
Club side: Manchester United
Previous Club: Bayern Munich
England Debut: 15.08.01, against Holland

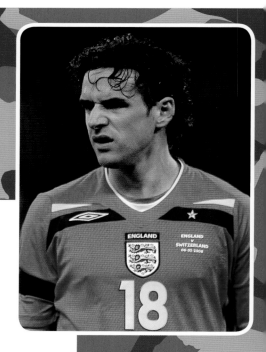

Even though Owen was born in Canada, he can still play for the Three Lions as his parents are English. Owen has amazing levels of stamina. The Man United man was named the England fans' Player of the Year in 2006, following impressive displays during that year's World Cup. His role as a deep-lying midfielder, shielding the defence and winning the ball back, allows the talents of Gerrard and Lampard to get further forward.

David Beckham

Born: 02.05.75, Leytonstone, London
Height: 6ft
Club side: LA Galaxy
Previous Clubs: Real Madrid, Preston North End (on loan), Manchester United
England Debut: 01.09.96, against Moldova

'Becks' is the only English player to have scored at three different World Cup tournaments and is one of the most famous footballers on the planet. He can strike a ball like nobody else, scoring spectacular free-kicks and supplying his team-mates with countless opportunities. Now playing in America with LA Galaxy, David is still at the top of his game and his style of play is very useful for England. He recently earned his 100th cap for England in a friendly against France on the 26th March 2008.

Player Profiles

Joe Cole

Born: 08.11.81, Islington, London
Height: 5ft 9in
Club side: Chelsea
Previous Club: West Ham
England Debut: 25.05.01, against Mexico

When he played for West Ham, Joe's nickname was 'The Conjuror' because of his amazing trickery with a football. Joe uses his superb skill to beat defenders and dribble the ball at a fast pace. The Chelsea man plays on the left for England, despite being right-footed, and creates great space for the Three Lions. Cole scored an awesome long-range volley goal against Sweden at the 2006 World Cup.

Peter Crouch

Born: 30.01.81, Macclesfield, Cheshire
Height: 6ft 7in
Club side: Liverpool
Previous Clubs: Include Southampton, Norwich City (on loan), Aston Villa, Portsmouth
England Debut: 31.05.05, against Colombia

Peter is the tallest player to ever play for the Three Lions. 'Crouchy' is one of England's most lethal strikers, with an excellent scoring record at international level.

Player Profiles

Jermain Defoe

Born: 07.10.82, Beckton, London
Height: 5ft 7in
Club side: Portsmouth
Previous Clubs: Tottenham Hotspur,
AFC Bournemouth (on loan), West Ham
England Debut: 31.03.04, against Sweden

Jermain scored in ten successive League games when he was on loan at Bournemouth. The Pompey striker uses his great balance and lightening quick speed to beat defenders and score.

Michael Owen

Born: 14.12.79, Chester
Height: 5ft 8in
Club side: Newcastle United
Previous Clubs: Real Madrid, Liverpool
England Debut: 11.02.98, against Chile

When England thrashed Germany 5-1 in 2001, Michael scored a hat-trick. He is one of the best strikers in the world and has an excellent goalscoring record for England. The Newcastle man can score with either foot, as well as his head. Michael has been starring for his country since he was 18 years old.

Player Profiles

Wayne Rooney

Born: 24.10.85, Liverpool
Height: 5ft 10in
Club side: Manchester United
Previous Club: Everton
England Debut: 12.02.03, against Australia

'Wazza' became England's youngest ever goalscorer in 2003. He was just 17 years and 317 days old. Wayne is a naturally talented player. He has fantastic pace, strength and skill, and can score goals from almost anywhere. He links the midfield to the attack perfectly by creating space and playing accurate passes. 'The Roon' has the ability to be one of the greatest England players of all time.

Gareth Barry

Born: 23.02.81, Hastings
Height: 6ft
Club side: Aston Villa
Previous Club: None
England Debut: 31.05.00, against Ukraine

When Gareth Barry played against Spain in 2007, it was his first international appearance in four years. Gareth is one of the most versatile performers in the England squad. The Aston Villa man can play in the centre of defence, as a full-back or in midfield. Barry possesses a deadly accurate left foot, excellent passing ability and an impressive work rate.

Player Profiles

David Bentley

Born: 27.08.84, Peterborough
Height: 5ft 8in
Club side: Blackburn Rovers
Previous Clubs: Norwich City (on loan), Arsenal
England Debut: 08.09.07, against Israel

David became the first Englishman to score at the new Wembley Stadium for the England Under-21s against their Italian counterparts on 24 March 2007. Bentley has a bright future on the international stage, having already shown he has the composure and ability to influence games at the highest level. A potential long-term successor to David Beckham on the right of midfield, much like Becks, he provides excellent delivery with crosses and free-kicks and can score spectacular long-range goals.

Wes Brown

Born: 13.10.79, Manchester
Height: 6ft 1in
Club side: Manchester United
Previous Club: None
England Debut: 28.04.99, against Hungary

Wes has been a regular in the England squad for almost a decade. A natural defender capable of performing at right-back or centrally, he is a reliable and committed performer for both club and country. The Manchester United man is tough in the tackle, strong in the air and an excellent man-marker.

Player Profiles

Michael Carrick

Born: 28.07.81, Wallsend, Tyne and Wear
Height: 6ft 2in
Club side: Manchester United
Previous Clubs: Tottenham Hotspur, Birmingham City (on loan), Swindon Town (on loan), West Ham
England Debut: 25.05.01, against Mexico

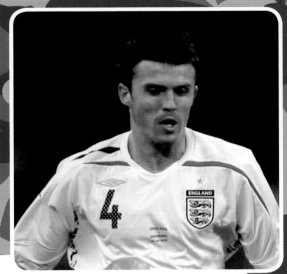

Michael's first start for the England team came against the USA on 28 May 2005. An excellent passer of the ball and one of the most composed and intelligent midfielders in England, Michael Carrick provides a different option for coach Fabio Capello. Operating in a deeper midfield role, he breaks up play with good reading of the game and sets attacks in motion with top class long and short-range passing.

Stewart Downing

Born: 22.07.84, Middlesbrough
Height: 5ft 11in
Club side: Middlesbrough
Previous Club: Sunderland (on loan)
England Debut: 09.02.05, against Holland

One of Stewart's early England matches came against Greece in 2006. The Three Lions won 4-0 and Downing set up three of the goals. Stewart is a rarity in the England squad – a naturally left-footed attacking winger. The Middlesbrough man provides pace, trickery and top-class crossing ability.

21

Emile Heskey

Born: 11.01.78, Leicester
Height: 6ft 2in
Club side: Wigan Athletic
Previous Clubs: Birmingham City, Liverpool, Leicester City
England Debut: 28.04.99, against Hungary

During his spell at Liverpool, Emile won two League Cups, one FA Cup and one UEFA Cup. Powerful, quick and physically imposing, Heskey is a real bulldozer of a centre-forward. The much-travelled striker is a tireless worker and his movement and strength create countless chances for his team-mates.

Jermaine Jenas

Born: 18.02.83, Nottingham
Height: 5ft 11in
Club side: Tottenham Hotspur
Previous Clubs: Newcastle United, Nottingham Forest
England Debut: 12.02.03, against Australia

Jermaine was voted the 2002-03 PFA Young Player of the Year. Jenas is developing into one of the best all-round midfielders in England and has established himself as a regular in the international squad. Energetic and as good going forward as he is defending, Jermaine also has the knack of scoring important goals.

Player Profiles

Andy Johnson

Born: 10.02.81, Bedford
Height: 5ft 7in
Club side: Everton
Previous Clubs: Crystal Palace, Birmingham City
England Debut: 09.02.05, against Holland

Andy joined Everton in 2006 and is contracted to the Blues until 2012. A real workaholic of a centre-forward, Andy Johnson is one of the most committed strikers in the Premiership. AJ's excellent running off the ball and desire to chase lost causes have led to plenty of chances for him and his colleagues. He is a neat finisher in front of goal with either foot.

John Terry

Born: 07.12.80, Barking, London
Height: 6ft 1in
Club side: Chelsea
Previous Club: Nottingham Forest (on loan)
England Debut: 03.06.03, against Serbia & Montenegro

John Terry was named as Steve McClaren's England captain in August 2006. John Terry is the man that England fans and players look to for inspiration. He is one of the best defenders in the world and any striker would fear playing against him. His strength, bravery and ability to score goals are vital for the England team.

23

Player Profiles

Micah Richards

Born: 24.06.88, Birmingham
Height: 5ft 11in
Club side: Manchester City
Previous Club: None
England Debut: 15.11.06, against Holland

When Micah made his England debut against Holland in 2006, he became the youngest ever defender to represent the Three Lions, aged just 18 years and 144 days. Richards is a natural athlete and one of the most promising defenders in the Premiership. Able to play as a full-back or centre-half, Micah uses his pace, strength and awesome aerial ability to good effect in an England shirt.

Shaun Wright-Phillips

Born: 25.10.81, Greenwich, London
Height: 5ft 6in
Club side: Chelsea
Previous Club: Manchester City
England Debut: 18.08.04, against Ukraine

Shaun is one of the few current England stars to have scored on his international debut after scoring his first goal for England against the Ukraine at St. James' Park in 2004. He is one of England's most dangerous attacking players and uses his awesome acceleration, pace and low centre of gravity to beat markers for fun. The Chelsea winger has added end product to his game in recent years and can boast an impressive scoring record at international level.

Positions

ENGLAND

Check out the football trivia, statistics and player debut info for each position on the pitch. Learn about the technical skills involved for all player positions and read up on the top tips so you can play like an England star.

Positions
Goalkeeper Trivia

Here are some interesting facts, trivia and stats about the men between the sticks.

Paul Robinson has scored two goals in his career so far. His first came for Leeds United against Swindon Town in a League Cup tie in 2003. The second was against another England international goalie, Ben Foster, when Robinson scored directly from a free-kick for Spurs against Watford in 2007. He actually took the kick from near the edge of his own area!

When **Chris Kirkland** made his England debut in 2006, his father was a happy man for more than one reason. Years earlier, he had placed a bet that his son would play for the senior team at odds of 100-1.

Robert Green made his England debut against Colombia in the USA in 2005. England won the game 3-2.

Scott Carson was once the record appearance holder for the England Under-21s, with 29 caps.

Peter Shilton is England's most capped player. The former Leicester City, Derby County and Nottingham Forest stopper played 125 times for his country.

David James holds the record for the most clean sheets in Premier League history. The Portsmouth man took over from David Seaman's record of 141, when he kept his 142nd clean sheet in 2007.

Ben Foster was a chef before he made it as a professional footballer.

David Seaman's nickname was 'Safe Hands'.

ENGL

Here are three top goalkeeper debut statistics.
Place the correct player sticker in the boxes.

Paul Robinson

DATE: 12 February 2003
OPPONENTS: Australia
VENUE: Upton Park, England
SCORE: England 1
        Australia 3

Scott Carson

DATE: 16 November 2007
OPPONENTS: Austria
VENUE: Ernst Happel
Stadium, Vienna
SCORE: England 1
        Austria 0

David James

DATE: 29 March 1997
OPPONENTS: Mexico
VENUE: Wembley, England
SCORE: England 2
        Mexico 0

GOALKEEPING TECHNIQUES

Agility to make dives and leaps, fast reactions and excellent handling skills are all things a good goalkeeper needs. Being in the right place at the right time is perhaps the goalkeeper's most important skill and probably the most difficult to learn. Good judgement only comes with experience and lots of work in training. Check out these top goalkeeping skills and tips.

Ready position

For a ready position, you should be well-balanced on the balls of your feet and prepared to move quickly in any direction. Hands should be held out at waist height.

Shot stopping

You should get as much of your body behind the ball as possible. Two hands are better than one, and it's also best if your body is positioned behind your hands to provide a second barrier. Getting any part of your body in front of the ball is important, whether it's one hand, your fingertips or an outstretched leg.

Low shots

For shots between knee and waist height, get the body behind the ball and use the scooping technique to bring it into the chest.

High balls

Catch the ball at the highest possible point – maximum height is gained with a one-footed take-off. Spread your fingers wide and bring the ball into your chest straight away.

Shots at chest height

There are two techniques:
1) Cup your hands underneath the ball and bend your body to clutch the ball into your chest.
2) Catch the ball with your fingers spread out and away from your body. Keep your fingers flexible at all times.

27

Positions
Defender Trivia

Read up on these facts about some of England's best defenders.

When he made his England debut against Holland in 2006, **Micah Richards** became England's youngest ever defender. Micah was 18 years and 144 days old and England drew the game 1-1.

Phil Neville's England debut came against China in 1996. He was 19 years old and England won the game 3-0.

John Terry was named Steve McClaren's England captain in August 2006, succeeding previous skipper David Beckham.

Rio Ferdinand's first goal for England came against Denmark at the 2002 World Cup. England won the game 3-0.

Ledley King scored his first goal for England on his third appearance, which was against Portugal in 2004.

Stuart Pearce's last game for England came against Poland in 1999. He was 37 years old.

Tony Adams played 66 times for England and scored five goals.

Ashley Cole played in all England's matches at Euro 2004 and the 2002 and 2006 World Cup Finals.

Terry Butcher won 77 caps for England and scored three goals.

ENGL

Here are three top defender debut statistics.
Place the correct player sticker in the boxes.

Rio Ferdinand

DATE: 15 November 1997
OPPONENTS: Cameroon
VENUE: Wembley, England
SCORE: England 2
        Cameroon 0

Ledley King

DATE: 27 March 2002
OPPONENTS: Italy
VENUE: Elland Road, England
SCORE: England 1
        Italy 2

Wes Brown

DATE: 28 April 1999
OPPONENTS: Hungary
VENUE: Budapest
SCORE: England 1
        Hungary 1

DEFENDING TECHNIQUES

Defending involves decision-making and taking up positions that will help your team win the ball or prevent your opponents from using it to their advantage. As a defender, you must try and stay between the opponent and your own goal to make it harder for the opponent to shoot. Here are some top skills and tips on defending.

Prevent your opponent from turning

A player receiving the ball will be a greater attacking threat if allowed to turn. As a defender, you should react quickly and get within one metre of your opponent by the time the ball arrives.

Tackling

Watch the ball, not the player. Keep moving yourself into the best position while you are waiting for the right moment to strike. When you decide to make a tackle, the important factors are speed, determination, accuracy and timing.

Jockeying

Wait for the attacker to momentarily lose control of the ball – don't dive in unnecessarily. Standing on the balls of his feet, the defender jockeys his opponent. His body weight is over his knees, which are flexed, and he is ready to move in any direction.

The slide tackle

Try to stay on your feet when tackling. Most players use the leg furthest away from the attacker to make the tackle as this gives you more balance. If your timing is good, hook your foot around the ball and cradle it there throughout the tackle to keep possession.

The block tackle

Ensure a good body position with your weight over the ball. Get as much of your foot in contact with the ball as possible and drive it through the tackling leg.

29

Check out these facts and stats about England's middle men.

Scott Parker made his England debut against Denmark in 2003. The Three Lions lost the game 2-3.

Joe Cole was only 19 years old when he made his England debut against Mexico in 1997.

Owen Hargreaves was voted as the England fans' Player of the Year in 2006, after his impressive performances at that year's World Cup.

Paul Scholes scored a hat-trick for England against Poland in 1999. England won the game 3-1.

Steven Gerrard scored his first goal for England in 2001, when the Three Lions beat Germany 5-1.

Nicky Butt was named as England's Best Player of the 2002 World Cup by Brazilian legend, Pele.

When he scored a trademark free-kick against Ecuador at the 2006 World Cup, **David Beckham** became the first ever Englishman to score at three different World Cups. His other goals came in the 1998 and 2002 tournaments.

Now with Hull City, **Nick Barmby** played 23 times for England and scored four goals.

In the 62 games he played for England, **David Platt** scored an impressive 27 goals.

ENGL

Here are three top defender debut statistics.
Place the correct player sticker in the boxes.

David Beckham

DATE: 1 September 1996
OPPONENTS: Moldova
VENUE: Republican Stadium
SCORE: England 3
      Moldova 0

Jermaine Jenas

DATE: 12 February 2003
OPPONENTS: Australia
VENUE: Upton Park, England
SCORE: England 1
      Australia 3

Steven Gerrard

DATE: 31 May 2000
OPPONENTS: Ukraine
VENUE: Wembley, England
SCORE: England 2
      Ukraine 0

MIDFIELDER TECHNIQUES

Check out these top tips for when you're playing midfield.

Shielding the ball

This action is vital when you have an opponent closing you down. The golden rule is to keep your body between your opponent and the ball, thereby making it much more difficult for them to make a tackle without committing a foul.

To shield the ball, position your body between the ball and your opponent.

Be aware of where your opponent is, and keep moving to ensure that your body stays between them and the ball. Keep your arms out for balance and look for your next move.

Throw-ins

Bend your knees and arch your back while keeping good balance.

Take the ball right back over your head.

Spread your hands around the back and sides of the ball so that your thumbs almost touch, so you have a good grip.

Release the ball as it passes in front of your head.

Remember to keep both feet on the ground, otherwise it's a foul throw.

As soon as you have taken the throw-in, step back onto the pitch and be alert.

Make life as easy as possible for the receiver. Your team-mate won't appreciate a ball bounding awkwardly or delivered where their marker can easily challenge.

Corners

Corners can be taken short or long and can be delivered to the far post, near post or middle of the goal. They can be bent inwards (inswing), or hit so that they bend outwards (outswing). Much depends on the corner taker to deliver an accurate ball at the right height, and into the right area, for his team.

Positions
Winger Trivia

Discover these great facts about England's wingers, past and present.

Shaun Wright-Phillips scored on his England debut against the Ukraine in August 2004.

Steve McManaman won the European Champions League twice whilst playing for Spanish super club Real Madrid.

Theo Walcott became England's youngest ever player when he made his England debut in 2006. The Arsenal man was only 17 years and 75 days old when he came on as a second-half substitute against Hungary at Old Trafford.

Former Liverpool legend **John Barnes**, who played 79 times for England, was actually born in Jamaica.

David Beckham once scored a goal from inside his own half whilst playing for Manchester United. Becks' spectacular effort came against Wimbledon at Selhurst Park in 1996.

Former Manchester United star **Lee Sharpe** only played eight times for England. He made his international debut against the Republic of Ireland in 1991.

In his 62 appearances for England, **Chris Waddle** scored six goals.

Aaron Lennon made his England debut against Jamaica in 2006. The Three Lions won the game at Old Trafford 6-0.

England's 1966 World Cup winning side were nicknamed the 'Wingless Wonders', as Alf Ramsey's side played with four more central midfielders in a very narrow system.

ENGL

Here are three top winger debut statistics.
Place the correct player sticker in the boxes.

David Bentley

DATE: 8 September 2007
OPPONENTS: Israel
VENUE: Wembley, England
SCORE: England 3
          Israel 0

Stewart Downing

DATE: 9 February 2005
OPPONENTS: Holland
VENUE: Villa Park, England
SCORE: England 0
          Holland 0

Joe Cole

DATE: 25 May 2001
OPPONENTS: Mexico
VENUE: Pride Park, England
SCORE: England 4
          Mexico 0

WINGER TECHNIQUES

Here are some great technical skills for when you're playing in a winger position.

Receiving the ball

Cushion control

This is used to control the ball's speed and keep it within your own playing distance. The part of your body making contact with the ball must be relaxed and must be moved away from the ball as it arrives to deaden its impact and leave it, usually, at your feet.

Firm control

Sometimes, players choose to keep some of the pace on the ball but change its direction. Firm control allows you to make an instant short pass to a team-mate or propel the ball ahead of you to run on to. The surface touching the ball should be held relatively firm and thrust forward on impact, for example, when you want to keep the ball moving ahead of you.

Controlling the ball

Whether you choose cushion or firm control, the same rules apply. Decide which part of the body you're going to use to receive the ball as early as possible. Get your body in line with the ball. Use your body to shield the ball from your marker and be aware of what is going on around you. This only comes with experience and lots of practice.

Dribbling

Dribbling is all about using close control skills with the ball to take on and beat one or more opponents. The more you can keep your opponent guessing, the better your chances of getting past them.

Keep the ball under close control. Kicking the ball too far ahead makes the defender's job easy.

Keep your head up. Keep an eye on the whereabouts of your team-mates and opponents.

Attack with pace. Make sure you vary your pace at times to keep the defender guessing.

33

Check out these great facts about England's strikers, past and present.

When **Michael Owen** netted three goals in the Three Lions' famous 5-1 thrashing of Germany in 2001, he became the first England player to score a hat-trick against the Germans since Geoff Hurst in 1966, when England won the World Cup.

Alan Shearer holds the record for most Premiership goals scored. The former England captain scored 260 goals in the country's top division.

Wayne Rooney holds the record for being England's youngest scorer. The Manchester United striker netted against Macedonia in 2003 when he was just 17 years and 317 days old.

Teddy Sheringham holds the record for most substitute appearances for England. The much-travelled striker was brought on 21 times during his Three Lions career.

When **Michael Owen** made his debut against Chile in 1998 aged 18 years and 59 days, he became England's youngest player of the 20th century.

Gary Lineker claimed the Golden Ball at the 1986 World Cup in Mexico after finishing the tournament's top scorer with six strikes. Gary's goals came against Poland, Paraguay and Argentina.

Jermain Defoe scored in ten consecutive League games whilst on loan at AFC Bournemouth in the 2000/01 season. He equalled John Aldridge's record in the process.

Gary Lineker missed out on levelling Sir Bobby Charlton's all-time England scoring record by just one goal. Lineker ended on 48 and Charlton scored 49.

Jimmy Greaves can boast an awesome striker record whilst on England duty. He scored an amazing 44 goals in 57 appearances. Greaves also notched up a record six hat-tricks for the Three Lions.

ENGL

Here are three top striker debut statistics.
Place the correct player sticker in the boxes.

Wayne Rooney
DATE: 12 February 2003
OPPONENTS: Australia
VENUE: Upton Park, England
SCORE: England 1
       Australia 3

Michael Owen
DATE: 11 February 1998
OPPONENTS: Chile
VENUE: Wembley, England
SCORE: England 0
       Chile 2

Peter Crouch
DATE: 31 May 2005
OPPONENTS: Colombia
VENUE: Giants Stadium, England
SCORE: England 3
       Colombia 2

STRIKER TECHNIQUES

Check out these great techniques for when you're playing as a striker.

Penalties

A penalty taker has a number of choices to make about where to hit the ball.

Some players prefer power; blasting the ball aimed at the middle of the goal. Others prefer to use a controlled instep drive low into the corners of the net.

Free-kicks

When it comes to deciding whether to shoot, the distance from goal and the angle will be the deciding factors. If the kick is too wide or too far out, then you should aim to get the ball into the danger area. This means you'll put pressure on the last defender.

Shooting

If an opportunity to shoot arises, and it is within your range, then go for it. Follow this checklist for shooting success:

Be aware
Keep your head up and your mind on the game.

Confidence is key
Don't be afraid of failure. If you miss, put it out of your mind and stay confident for next time.

Be quick
Chances come and go in an instant. Don't hesitate or take one touch too many.

Go low
Aiming high towards the top corner of the goal may look good, but there's also a good chance of it being saved or soaring over the goalposts. A low shot can be more effective and may also lead to a deflection.

Placement versus power
For close-range shooting, accuracy comes first and power second. Even if you are taking a shot from further out, concentrate on a smooth swing of the foot rather than smashing the ball.

35

Activities

Here's a great selection of games, puzzles and quizzes that will test your England football knowledge to the max. Get playing the game!

Activities
Footballer Wordsearch

Find the surnames of the 20 England stars listed below.
Look forwards, backwards, vertically, horizontally
and diagonally.

Q	B	Y	Q	V	Z	X	V	J	G	N	U	O	Y	W
H	P	N	H	S	P	K	V	J	N	E	J	N	O	A
Y	W	O	B	E	Z	M	X	S	J	E	L	O	C	K
Y	G	Y	M	V	R	Y	F	C	S	R	D	S	J	Q
D	V	E	M	A	D	F	Y	C	C	G	U	N	Y	A
U	E	N	R	E	X	S	D	R	A	H	C	I	R	S
F	G	O	F	R	V	W	P	T	M	H	A	B	I	A
W	S	O	F	G	A	B	E	I	P	B	R	O	W	N
Y	E	R	G	R	N	R	E	B	B	R	R	R	E	E
P	T	D	N	A	N	I	D	R	E	F	I	O	E	J
H	E	H	I	H	H	D	N	G	L	C	C	P	F	E
V	F	Q	K	L	S	G	Y	W	L	M	K	W	Q	S
Z	K	G	N	R	W	E	C	R	O	U	C	H	H	I
U	I	Y	P	O	L	M	O	F	G	D	E	L	A	U
A	M	C	P	O	G	V	O	P	P	K	B	O	R	M

BECKHAM	DEFOE	KING
BRIDGE	DOWNING	RICHARDS
BROWN	FERDINAND	ROBINSON
CAMPBELL	GERRARD	ROONEY
CARRICK	GREEN	WOODGATE
COLE	HARGREAVES	YOUNG
CROUCH	JENAS	

38

Activities
Spot the Ball

Guess where the ball is in the footy action photo below. Use the letters running vertically and horizontally along the grid to give your answer.

Matthew Upson battles for the ball.

	A	B	C	D	E	F
1						
2						
3						
4						
5						
6						

39

Activities
True or False

See if you can work out if the following statements are true or false.

1. Gary Lineker used to play for Spanish side Valencia.   **True/False**

2. Terry Venables was England manager when David Beckham made his England debut.   **True/False**

3. Michael Owen once scored a handball goal for England.   **True/False**

4. David Beckham's first game as captain of England was against Italy.   **True/False**

5. Ashley Cole used to be a striker.   **True/False**

6. The 2008 European Championship will be held in Russia.   **True/False**

7. Jermaine Jenas started his career at Leicester City.   **True/False**

8. England's first goal of the 2002 World Cup was scored by Sol Campbell.   **True/False**

9. Shaun Wright-Phillips has never scored for England.   **True/False**

10. Wayne Rooney made his England debut against Australia.   **True/False**

ENGLAND

Can you identify the players in these four blurry pictures?

1. ....

2. ....

3. ....

4. ....

41

Activities
Spot the Difference

Examine the football action scene below and see if you can find six differences in the bottom picture.

Activities
Stadium Anagrams

ENGL

Look at the list below of some of the famous football stadiums around the world. They have been jumbled up – can you identify the correct stadium names?

1. DLO FFARDORT

2. ONU PAMC

3. NAS RISO

4. NERBUBEA

5. FANDLIE

6. BLEMWEY

7. FOSTRAMD GIRBED

8. SETLALAM

9. DASTIO EDLAL PILA

10. STAMERMAD ERANA

11. DESTA DOMELVORE

12. CARANAMA

13. DASET RAFANICS

14. PANDEMH RAPK

15. LELIMMNUNI DISATUM

43

Activities
Footy Crossword

Check out your knowledge of the game in this footy crossword by answering the clues below, and completing the grid on the opposite page.

ACROSS

2. Theo Walcott's club (7)
4. Ferdinand's first name (3)
5. Losing finalists in 1966 (7)
8. Italia '90 star David ... (5)
11. England legend ... Pearce (6)
12. Former England boss, Glenn ... (6)
14. Michael Owen's club, ... United (9)
16. Former England boss, Bobby ... (6)
18. Chelsea star, Frank ... (7)
20. Alan Smith's first club, ... United (5)

DOWN

1. Wigan keeper, Chris ... (8)
3. Chelsea winger, Shaun ... (14)
6. Carrick's first name (7)
7. Young keeper, Scott ... (6)
9. Liverpool striker, Peter ... (6)
10. Luke Young's club (13)
13. Defender ... Brown (3)
15. Goals Wayne Bridge has scored (3)
17. Pompey keeper, ... James (5)
19. Midfielder, Kieron ... (4)

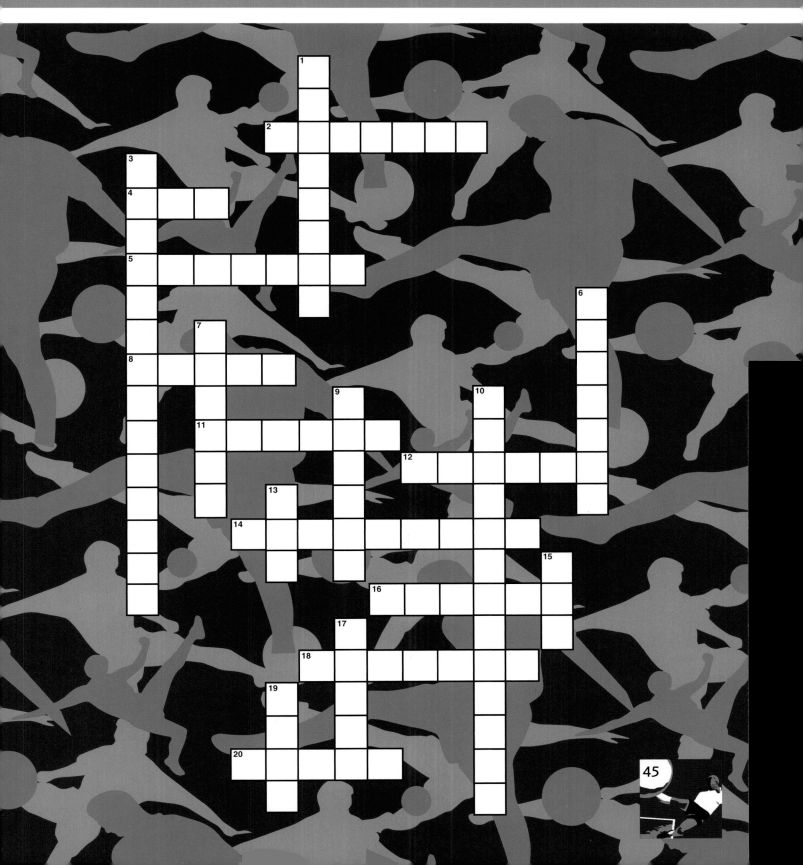

Design a kit

As you know, England play in white shirts with navy blue shorts and white socks. Add in the Three Lions on the crest and you've got one of the most famous football kits in the world.

Now have a go at designing your own England kit. Simply photocopy this page and away you go. Perhaps you could even have a competition with your friends at school and ask your teacher to choose the best one!

46

Use the Three Lions symbol to come up with a new England badge.
Use the space below to draw your design.

ENGLAND

47

Activities
England Trivia Quiz

This is the ultimate test for all England fans! Take this quiz to find out how clued up you are on your favourite game.

1. Which country is England manager Fabio Capello from?

....

2. Who did David Beckham score his first goal against?

....

3. Which country hosted Euro 2004?

....

4. Name the three English clubs that former England boss Kevin Keegan has managed.

....

5. Who was England manager for the 1998 World Cup?

....

6. Who scored more goals for England, David Platt or Alan Shearer?

....

7. Which midfielder scored England's second goal against Trinidad and Tobago at the 2006 World Cup?

....

8. Who scored a hat-trick in England's 5-1 win over Germany in 2001?

....

9. Which Aston Villa player earned a recall to the England squad in 2007 after a four-year absence?

....

10. Which player scored the last ever international goal at the old Wembley stadium?

....

11. What was Frank Lampard's first ever club?

....

12. How many goals did England score in the 1966 World Cup Final?

....

13. What's the furthest stage England have ever reached at the European Championship?

....

14. How old was Stewart Downing when he made his England debut?

....

15. Which former England star is now playing for League One side AFC Bournemouth ?

....

16. Who played for England first, Steven Gerrard or Frank Lampard?

....

17. Which England defender is the captain of Everton?

....

18. Who holds the record of most caps earned for England?

....

19. Which England left-back plays for Reading?

....

20. Who is England's top scorer of all time?

....

Which clubs do these England stars play for?

1. Steven Gerrard
2. Ashley Cole
3. Michael Carrick
4. David James
5. Stewart Downing
6. Emile Heskey
7. Frank Lampard
8. David Bentley
9. Phil Neville
10. Micah Richards
11. Paul Robinson
12. Wayne Rooney
13. Ashley Young
14. Ledley King
15. Alan Smith

Activities
Match the Club

How well do you know your football clubs? See if you can match the clubs to their nicknames, by drawing a line to join them up.

THE LATICS

POMPEY

THE RED DEVILS

THE MAGPIES

THE HAMMERS

THE GUNNERS

SPURS

THE VILLANS

THE REDS

THE BLUES

WIGAN ATHLETIC

MANCHESTER UNITED

PORTSMOUTH

WEST HAM

NEWCASTLE UNITED

BIRMINGHAM CITY

LIVERPOOL

TOTTENHAM HOTSPUR

ASTON VILLA

ARSENAL

Activities
Answers

Page 38: Footballer Wordsearch

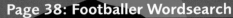

Page 39: Spot the Ball: A2

Page 40: True or False

1. False	6. False
2. False	7. False
3. False	8. True
4. True	9. False
5. True	10. True

Page 41: Guess the Player

1. Owen Hargreaves
2. Joe Cole
3. Peter Crouch
4. David Beckham

Page 42: Spot the Difference

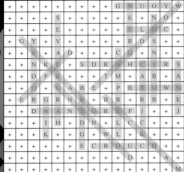

Page 43: Stadium Anagrams

1. Old Trafford
2. Nou Camp
3. San Siro
4. Bernabeu
5. Anfield
6. Wembley
7. Stamford Bridge
8. Mestalla
9. Stadio Della Alpi
10. Amsterdam Arena
11. Stade Velodrome
12. Maracana
13. Stade Francais
14. Hampden Park
15. Millennium Stadium

Pages 44-45: Footy Crossword

Pages 48-49: England Trivia Quiz

1. Italy
2. Colombia
3. Portugal
4. Newcastle, Fulham, Man City
5. Glenn Hoddle
6. Alan Shearer
7. Steven Gerrard
8. Michael Owen
9. Gareth Barry
10. Dietmar Hamann
11. West Ham
12. Four
13. The semi-finals
14. 20 years old
15. Darren Anderton
16. Frank Lampard
17. Phil Neville
18. Peter Shilton
19. Nicky Shorey
20. Sir Bobby Charlton

Page 50: Players and Clubs

1. Liverpool
2. Chelsea
3. Manchester United
4. Portsmouth
5. Middlesbrough
6. Wigan
7. Chelsea
8. Blackburn
9. Everton
10. Manchester City
11. Tottenham Hotspur
12. Manchester United
13. Aston Villa
14. Tottenham Hotspur
15. Newcastle United

Page 51: Match the Club

The Latics – Wigan Athletic, Pompey – Portsmouth
The Red Devils – Manchester United, The Magpies
– Newcastle United, The Hammers – West Ham,
The Gunners – Arsenal, Spurs – Tottenham Hotspur
The Villans – Aston Villa, The Reds – Liverpool,
The Blues – Birmingham City.

Great Games

Take a close-up look at ten of the most thrilling England games of all time, from the 1966 World Cup to playing against England's old rivals, Argentina, in 2005. See if your favourite game is among them.

Great Games
Portugal 1966

The occasion:
World Cup Semi-final, Wembley, 26 July 1966

Who's playing?
England v Portugal

Score: England 2, Portugal 1

As the country began to dream of England's first World Cup Final, Alf Ramsey and his men were fully focused on the threat provided by Portugal in the semi-finals. The Portuguese were a technically gifted team filled with plenty of class acts, including super strikers Eusebio and Jose Torres.

During a tight first-half, England had enjoyed plenty of possession but failed to create many clear-cut chances, and Eusebio was looking dangerous in attack. With half an hour played, Bobby Charlton rattled the ball into the back of the net after Roger Hunt's shot rebounded back off the Portuguese keeper to give England a vital lead.

In the second half, the Three Lions continued to press forward but still defended stoutly, with Nobby Stiles marking dangerman Eusebio extremely tightly.

England goalkeeper Gordon Banks punches the ball clear.

With just over ten minutes of play remaining, Geoff Hurst latched onto a long ball from Stiles and held off the challenge of his marker before laying the ball back to Bobby Charlton. Without hesitation, Charlton slammed the ball into the corner of the goal with awesome power and gave England a two goal lead.

Eusebio fired home a penalty three minutes later to keep English nerves jangling, but the defence held strong and Alf Ramsey's men reached the final with Charlton the hero.

Great Games
World Cup 1966

The occasion:
World Cup Final, Wembley, 30 July 1966

Who's playing:
England v West Germany

Score: England 4, Germany 2

Germany started off as slight favourites, so it was no surprise when they took the lead after just 12 minutes. But England were soon back in it, with Geoff Hurst heading home a free-kick from the England skipper Bobby Moore. And it stayed at 1-1 until 12 minutes from the end.

Martin Peters then put England back into the lead, tapping home from close range. The Wembley crowd went mad but then disaster struck. Germany won a free-kick, the ball cannoned off the wall and fell to the German defender Wolfgang Weber, who slotted it past the England keeper Gordon Banks to make it 2-1 to Germany.

When it came to extra time it all became very controversial. A shot by Hurst hit the underside of the bar and bounced down. "But did it cross the goal line?", the referee asked the linesman. They had a brief chat and then the referee pointed towards the centre circle. Goal! England were 3-2 up.

This time, the Germans failed to come back. With the last kick of the game, Hurst scored and became the first player to score a hat-trick (three goals) in a World Cup Final. England were World Champions.

England captain Bobby Moore holds the World Cup aloft as he is carried by his jubilant team-mates.

55

Great Games
Cameroon 1990

The occasion:
World Cup Quarter-final, 1 July 1990

Who's playing?
England v Cameroon

Score: England 3, Cameroon 2

England's John Barnes on the attack.

David Platt scored the only goal of the first half, heading home a Stuart Pearce cross. But although Cameroon had plenty of chances to draw level, Peter Shilton and the rest of the England defence just about stood firm.

At the start of the second half, England finally cracked, with Paul Gascoigne fouling Cameroon star Roger Milla in the box.

The resulting penalty levelled the score sheet at 1-1. England began to look a bit creaky and within five minutes of their first goal the Africans were ahead 2-1.

Things were not going to plan at all. The English midfield were being over-run and half the defence was limping. Time was ticking away. With seven minutes left, in a last ditch attempt to level the score, England hero Gary Lineker surged into the box but was sent flying. Penalty! Up stepped Lineker to make it 2-2 and take the game into extra time.

It ended with a fantastic finish. Paul Gascoigne split the defence with a perfect pass, and as Lineker ran into the box, the Cameroon keeper ran out to meet him, resulting in another penalty for the Three Lions. Once again the team's hopes rested with Lineker. Will he blast it or place? Go right or left? Lineker went straight down the middle...but the keeper went to his right, resulting in a 3-2 win, which propelled England into the semi-finals.

ENGLAND

The occasion:
European Championship Group Stage, Wembley, 15 June 1996

Who's playing?
England v Scotland

Score: England 2, Scotland 0

As a frustrating first half for the Three Lions came to end with the scores locked at 0-0, many England fans were concerned about their side's tournament chances. Scotland had battled well and enjoyed plenty of possession, defending stoutly and often out-numbering the English in midfield.

England manager Terry Venables brought on a young Jamie Redknapp at the beginning of the second half, and his accurate passing played a major role in England taking charge.

The first goal came after a surging right-flank run from Gary Neville, whose deep cross was finished off by the reliable head of Alan Shearer. Scotland refused to give in and after 76 minutes they earned a penalty after a rough Tony Adams tackle on Gordon Durie. Gary McAllister stepped up to take the shot, but halfway through his run up, the ball moved slightly on the penalty spot. He took the kick anyway, and David Seaman pulled off a fantastic save to maintain England's lead.

Paul Gascoigne celebrates his goal with Teddy Sheringham.

Just three minutes later, Gazza scored after clipping a Darren Anderton through-ball over his body and avoiding the challenge of Scottish defender Colin Hendry with his left foot. He then allowed the ball to drop, before catching it full on the volley with his right foot, beating goalkeeper Andy Goram's flailing dive to settle the match.

57

Great Games
Holland 1996

The occasion:
Group match, European Championship, Wembley, 18 June 1996

Who's playing?
England v Holland

Score: England 4, Holland 1

It started as Alan Shearer blasted England ahead from the penalty spot after Paul Ince had been tripped. But it wasn't until the second half that England upped the tempo and began purring like a finely tuned engine.

Darren Anderton's long shot was saved by the Dutch keeper Edwin Van Der Sar, but it squirmed free and Sheringham tucked home the rebound.

England were beginning to play football worthy of their reputation as one of the world's best teams. Teddy Sheringham headed in the second goal from a Paul Gascoigne corner, but the best was yet to come.

Steve McManaman passed to Gascoigne, who skipped past a defender before passing the ball to Teddy Sheringham. Everyone thought Teddy was going to shoot, but instead he slid the ball across the box to Shearer, who smashed home his second goal of the game.

Holland did get one back and that was enough to see them qualify for the next stage, knocking out Scotland in the process.

England's Paul Gascoigne in action.

Great Games
Germany 1996

ENGLAND

The occasion:
European Championship Semi-final, Wembley, 26 June 1996

Who's playing?
England v Germany

Score: England 1, Germany 1 (5-6 on penalties)

At the start, England got off to an absolute flyer when Alan Shearer headed home a near-post corner after just two minutes. It looked like it was going downhill after that…Germany equalised just over ten minutes later. But both teams held steady and there were no more goals, causing the game to go into extra time and then Golden Goals, with the next team to score the winners.

First, Darren Anderton was inches away with a shot that flew across the face of the goal. Then moments later, Stefan Kuntz scored for Germany at the other end. The 76,000 people who had crammed into Wembley looked at the referee; the referee looked at his linesman; the linesman looked back at him. "No goal," said the man in black. The game was still on!

Suddenly Shearer found himself out on the right wing. Racing up the pitch to the German goal, he passed to Paul Gascoigne, who slid in dramatically...but missed the ball. The referee blew the whistle, signalling that dreaded occasion: penalties.

Incredibly, England scored the first five but, unfortunately, so did Germany. So up stepped Gareth Southgate. As the nation watched, he ran forward and hit it too close to the keeper. Cue Andreas Möller, who stroked the ball past David Seaman and put Germany into the final.

England captain Tony Adams clashes with Germany's Andreas Möller during the Euro 96 Semi-final at Wembley.

Great Games
Argentina 1998

The occasion:
World Cup Second Round, Saint-Etienne, 30 June 1998

Who's playing?
England v Argentina

Score: England 2, Argentina 2 (3-4 on penalties)

Glenn Hoddle's England team had negotiated their qualifying group after a pair of 2-0 victories over Tunisia and Colombia, and were ready to up their game against the highly-rated Argentina side. The South Americans could boast the likes of Ariel Ortega and Gabriel Batistuta in their ranks, and were one of the most dangerous teams left in the competition.

The game was played at a ferocious pace, with both teams crunching into tackles and determined to attack. The Argentines struck first when, after just five minutes, Batistuta was felled in the area by David Seaman and the referee awarded a penalty. 'Batigol' dusted himself down to convert the penalty and take the early lead for his team. Five minutes later, Michael Owen was brought down in the box as the Argentine defence struggled to cope with his pace, and Alan Shearer stepped up to the spot to equalise with typical conviction.

England were now equal and Owen and Shearer could smell blood. After 15 minutes, Owen picked up the ball near the halfway line and began a blistering run through the heart of the

South Americans. Gliding past challenges, the teenager arrived in the area and drilled a deadly accurate strike into the roof of the net to give England the lead.

The Argentinians then began to dominate and, after plenty of possession, equalised on the stroke of half-time after Javier Zanetti finished off a clever free-kick. In the second half the game changed, when David Beckham was harshly sent off by referee Kim Milton Nielsen for retaliating to Diego Simone's wind-up tactics.

The brave ten Lions held on for extra time and penalties and could even have won the game, but Sol Campbell's header was ruled out for pushing. As Paul Ince and David Batty failed from the spot in the shoot-out, England crashed out of another World Cup. But they could return home with their heads held high after a memorable match and a courageous performance.

ENGLAND

The occasion:
World Cup Qualifier in Munich, 1 September 2001

Who's playing?
Germany v England

Score: England 5, Germany 1

Germany had a six-point lead at the top of the qualifying group for the 2002 World Cup and only one team were certain to go through.

Six minutes into the game, Carsten Jancker gave Germany the lead. But then England went on an incredible scoring spree. First, Michael Owen smashed home a tremendous half volley and then Steven Gerrard went one better, with an absolute screamer from 30 yards out. The England fans at the ground were going barmy!

As half-time approached, England's confidence was soaring and it wasn't long into the second half when Owen took advantage of the flagging German defence to bag his second goal, after a knock down from strike partner Emile Heskey. Owen then completed his hat-trick as his electric pace left Germany reeling and he launched the ball into the back of the net to make it 4-1.

The final blow to Germany was dealt by Emile Heskey, who scored to make it 5-1. It was Germany's worst defeat since they lost 6-0 to Austria in 1930.

61

England's Michael Owen (front) celebrates with Steven Gerrard after scoring against Germany.

Great Games
Portugal 2004

The occasion:
European Championship Quarter-final, Lisbon, 24 June 2004

Who's playing?
England v Portugal

Score: England 2, Portugal 2 (5-6 on penalties)

It started unbelievably well for England. David James launched a huge goal kick, which Michael Owen controlled brilliantly before flicking it over the keeper into the back of the net. England were one up with just three minutes on the clock.

Portugal didn't equalise straight away, and England managed to hold on until seven minutes from the final whistle. But then, Portuguese substitute Helder Postiga sneaked past the England defence to head the ball home. This meant extra time, but only after Sol Campbell had a perfectly good goal ruled out right on the final whistle. Instead it was Portugal who went ahead, this time through a fantastic strike by Rui Costa after 110 minutes.

England were down but not out yet. Displaying his technical supremacy, Frank Lampard stabbed the ball home from close range to keep England's hopes alive and send the match into penalties.

However, David Beckham slipped as he ran up to take the first kick and sent it over the bar.

At 5-5, Portuguese goalkeeper Ricardo saved well from Darius Vassell and then cruelly rubbed England's noses in it by stepping up to slot home the winner himself.

Portugal defeats England 6-5 on penalties in the quarter-finals of the Euro 2004 at the stadium in Lisbon, Portugal. England is eliminated.

ENGLAND

The occasion:
International Friendly, Stade de Geneve, Geneva, 12 November 2005

Who's playing?
England v Argentina

Score: England 3, Argentina 2

In David Beckham's 50th match as captain, England met their old rivals Argentina in Switzerland. The South Americans came to Europe with a very high reputation, and they soon showed exactly why, playing some superb one and two touch football, dominating the midfield and looking dangerous going forward. For once, a friendly match was taken extremely seriously, possibly because the neutral venue enhanced the atmosphere and the game, likening it to a World Cup contest.

Inspired by their outstanding playmaker Juan Roman Riquelme and exciting winger Maxi Rodriguez, Argentina took control of the game and took the lead through Hernan Crespo after 35 minutes. But Wayne Rooney grabbed an equaliser before half-time to level the scores and keep England in the game.

In the second half, defender Walter Samuel popped up with a header to regain the lead for Argentina and England looked to have just fallen short. Sven-Goran Eriksson threw caution to the wind and brought on Peter Crouch for defender Luke Young and went for broke. The Argentinian back four struggled to contain the Liverpool striker as he dragged them out of position and won everything in the air. The ensuing confusion was tailor-made for Michael Owen, who snapped up a brace of goals in the final minutes to turn the match on its head and give the players and supporters an inspiring victory.

63

England's Michael Owen celebrates scoring the winning goal as Argentina goalkeeper Roberto Abbondanzieri lies on the floor.

England Legends

Since 1945, many footballers have had the honour of representing England at international level. Some are now household names, whilst others have faded from memory. This selection of England players truly deserve the title 'legend'.

England Legends
Alan Shearer

NAME: Alan Shearer
DATE OF BIRTH: 13 August 1970
PLACE OF BIRTH: Gosforth, Newcastle
HEIGHT: 6ft
CLUBS: Southampton, Blackburn Rovers, Newcastle United
ENGLAND CAPS: 63
ENGLAND GOALS: 30
INTERNATIONAL DEBUT: Vs France in 1992
LAST INTERNATIONAL APPEARANCE: Vs Romania in 2000
INTERESTING INFO: Alan captained England on 34 occasions.

Alan Shearer was one of the finest English strikers ever to play for his country.

A classic target man, Shearer carved out a reputation for himself at Southampton before a move to Blackburn Rovers in 1993 saw him rise to stardom. He won the Premier League title with Blackburn in 1995 and established himself as one of the most feared strikers in England.

He starred for England in Euro 96 and finished as the tournament's top scorer with five goals. Alan left Blackburn to join his boyhood heroes Newcastle United after the tournament. Shearer was named England captain in 1998 and went on to represent England at the World Cup of that year and the 2000 European Championship. He is remembered for his consistency, work ethic and lethal finishing with both his feet and his head.

England captain Alan Shearer celebrates after scoring during a first round match against Germany at Charleroi in Belgium

NAME: Paul Scholes
DATE OF BIRTH: 16 November 1974
PLACE OF BIRTH: Salford
HEIGHT: 5ft 7in
CLUB: Manchester United
ENGLAND CAPS: 66
ENGLAND GOALS: 14
INTERNATIONAL DEBUT: Vs South Africa in 1997
LAST INTERNATIONAL APPEARANCE: Vs Portugal in 2004
INTERESTING INFO: Paul has made over 500 first team appearances for Manchester United and won seven Premiership titles whilst at Old Trafford.

Paul Scholes is one of the best English players of his generation. The Manchester United man first broke through into the first team at Old Trafford as a striker, but as the seasons went by his all-round attributes were better suited to an attacking midfield role. He has been the catalyst for much of Manchester United's success in the modern era. For England, Scholes will be remembered for scoring a hat-trick against Poland at Wembley in 1999, and the two vital goals he notched up against Scotland at Hampden Park in a European Championship qualification play-off in the same year.

Paul Scholes playing for England against Turkey in 2004.

67

England Legends
David Platt

NAME: David Platt

DATE OF BIRTH: 10 June 1966

PLACE OF BIRTH: Chadderton

HEIGHT: 5ft 10in

CLUBS: Crewe Alexandra, Aston Villa, Bari, Sampdoria, Juventus, Arsenal, Nottingham Forest

ENGLAND CAPS: 62

ENGLAND GOALS: 27

INTERNATIONAL DEBUT: Vs Italy in 1989

LAST INTERNATIONAL APPEARANCE: Vs Germany in 1996

INTERESTING INFO: David's last kick in an England shirt was the penalty he scored in the semi-final shoot-out against Germany at Euro 96.

David Platt contributed significantly to the success of the Three Lions. The former Aston Villa man weighed in with plenty of vital goals from midfield, including a classic volleyed winner in extra time against Belgium in the knock-out stage.

His performances at the 1990 World Cup led to a move to Italy with Bari. Platt also went on to play for Juventus and Sampdoria with great distinction and will go down as one of England's most successful players to play in a Foreign League. Platt captained his country on several occasions and produced a level of consistency that many players could only dream of.

England's David Platt celebrates scoring his penalty.

NAME: Bryan Robson
DATE OF BIRTH: 11 January 1957
PLACE OF BIRTH: Chester-le-Street
HEIGHT: 6ft
CLUBS: West Bromwich Albion, Manchester United, Middlesbrough
ENGLAND CAPS: 90
ENGLAND GOALS: 26
INTERNATIONAL DEBUT: Vs Republic of Ireland in 1980
LAST INTERNATIONAL APPEARANCE: Vs Turkey in 1991
INTERESTING INFO: Bryan is currently the sixth most capped English player of all time.

'Robbo' or 'Captain Marvel' was one of the finest players to wear an England shirt in the 1970s, 80s and 90s. Manchester United's midfield maestro was an inspirational leader for the Three Lions and his roving runs from box to box, incredible energy levels and strength in the tackle made him an awesome competitor. He was the complete central midfielder, with an ability to score goals with either foot and his head.

Robson's 'never say die' attitude often led to him playing whilst injured and he would have surely reached the 100 cap mark for his country if it wasn't for injury, which caused him to miss games in the 1986 and 1990 World Cups. Bryan will be remembered as an England great and a true football warrior.

Bryan Robson playing against Turkey in one of his last international appearances.

England Legends
Tony Adams

NAME: Tony Adams

DATE OF BIRTH: 10 October 1966

PLACE OF BIRTH: Romford

HEIGHT: 6ft 3in

CLUB: Arsenal

ENGLAND CAPS: 66

ENGLAND GOALS: 5

INTERNATIONAL DEBUT: Vs Spain in 1987

LAST INTERNATIONAL APPEARANCE: Vs Germany in 2000

INTERESTING INFO: Tony was named Arsenal's youngest ever club captain when he was awarded the armband aged just 21 in 1988.

Tony Adams was a true leader of men and real organiser at the heart of the England defence. The Arsenal legend was dominant in the air and fierce in the tackle, showing an ability to read what was happening on the pitch at the highest level.

Later in his career, Tony developed a better understanding of the game and his ability on the ball and range of passing improved remarkably. Adams was one of the stars of England's successful Euro 96 campaign when he formed a solid partnership with Gareth Southgate and always gave his all for the Three Lions.

Tony Adams prepares for England's Group A game against Portugal in Euro 2000.

ENGLAND

NAME: Stanley Matthews

DATE OF BIRTH: 1 February 1915

PLACE OF BIRTH: Hanley

HEIGHT: 5ft 8in

CLUBS: Stoke City, Blackpool

ENGLAND CAPS: 54

ENGLAND GOALS: 11

INTERNATIONAL DEBUT: Vs Wales in 1934

LAST INTERNATIONAL APPEARANCE: Vs Denmark in 1957

INTERESTING INFO: Matthews is England's oldest ever goalscorer. Stanley was 41 years and 248 days old when he struck against Northern Ireland in Belfast on 6 October 1956.

A supremely gifted and clever winger, Stanley Matthews was known as the 'Wizard of Dribble'. His game was filled with tricks and shimmies, and his skills left back-pedalling full-backs in a daze and swinging at fresh air as they attempted to make a tackle. Sir Stan will be remembered as one of the finest English players of all time and the inspiration for many of the players of the next generation, including the 1966 World Cup heroes.

71

Stanley Matthews getting ready for a friendly game against Hungary.

England Legends
Alan Ball

NAME: Alan Ball

DATE OF BIRTH: 12 May 1945

PLACE OF BIRTH: Farnworth

HEIGHT: 5ft 6in

CLUBS: Blackpool, Everton, Arsenal, Southampton, Philadelphia Fury, Vancouver Whitecaps, Eastern AA, Bristol Rovers

ENGLAND CAPS: 72

ENGLAND GOALS: 8

INTERNATIONAL DEBUT: Vs Yugoslavia in 1965

LAST INTERNATIONAL APPEARANCE: Vs Scotland in 1975

INTERESTING INFO: Alan was the youngest member of the 1966 World Cup squad, aged just 21.

It was as a teenager with Blackpool that Alan won his first England cap.

A terrier-like midfielder, whose awesome energy levels were crucial to England's 1966 World Cup success, Alan Ball was an energetic player with excellent passing ability. His pace, acceleration and natural balance allowed him to buzz past defenders and play dangerous balls into the box. Playing a more central role in 1966, Ball's work ethic and desire to link up with the forwards gave England width when they needed it, as illustrated when he set up Geoff Hurst's second goal in the final.

NAME: Stuart Pearce

DATE OF BIRTH: 24 April 1962

PLACE OF BIRTH: Hammersmith

HEIGHT: 5ft 10in

CLUBS: Wealdstone, Coventry City, Nottingham Forest, Newcastle United, West Ham United, Manchester City

ENGLAND CAPS: 78

ENGLAND GOALS: 5

INTERNATIONAL DEBUT: Vs Brazil in 1987

LAST INTERNATIONAL APPEARANCE: Vs Poland in 1999

INTERESTING INFO: Stuart is now the head coach of the England Under-21 side and a part of Fabio Capello's backroom staff.

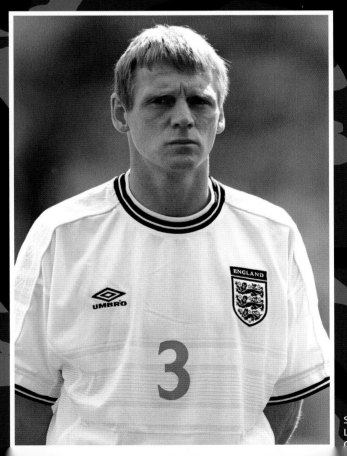

Whole-hearted, unflinching in the tackle and a tigerish competitor, Stuart Pearce's presence in the England defence provided extra bite and a superb natural balance. The tough-tackling left-back defended the England goal as though his life depended on it. Famously known as 'Psycho', the Nottingham Forest legend possessed a wickedly powerful left-foot shot and was one of the proudest men to have ever worn the Three Lions on his chest.

Stuart Pearce preparing to play Luxembourg in a Euro 2000 Qualifier

England Legends
Jimmy Greaves

NAME: Jimmy Greaves

DATE OF BIRTH: 20 February 1940

PLACE OF BIRTH: East Ham, London

HEIGHT: 5ft 8in

CLUBS: Chelsea, AC Milan, Tottenham Hotspur, West Ham United, Brentwood Town, Chelmsford City, Barnet

ENGLAND CAPS: 57

ENGLAND GOALS: 44

INTERNATIONAL DEBUT: Vs Peru in 1959

LAST INTERNATIONAL APPEARANCE: Vs Austria in 1967

INTERESTING INFO: Jimmy Greaves only played three more games for England after the 1966 World Cup Finals, adding just one further goal to his tally.

When Jimmy Greaves played for England, he usually scored, amassing a hugely impressive tally of 44 goals in 57 games, including six hat-tricks – a record that still stands today. Jimmy famously missed the 1966 Final after an injury earlier in the tournament ruled him out of the later stages and Geoff Hurst's fine form kept him out of the final. Probably England's most naturally talented striker and a deadly finisher, Jimmy Greaves is currently England's third highest scorer of all time.

Jimmy Greaves joined Chelsea in 1957 and in 1961 had a short spell with Milan before coming back to England and Spurs

ENGLAND

NAME: John Barnes

DATE OF BIRTH: 7 November 1963

PLACE OF BIRTH: Kingston, Jamaica

HEIGHT: 5ft 11in

CLUBS: Watford, Liverpool, Newcastle United, Charlton Athletic

ENGLAND CAPS: 79

ENGLAND GOALS: 11

INTERNATIONAL DEBUT: Vs Northern Ireland in 1983

LAST INTERNATIONAL APPEARANCE: Vs Colombia in 1995

INTERESTING INFO: Barnes famously rapped on England's 1990 World Cup theme song, 'World in Motion' by New Order.

John Barnes playing in the US Cup against the USA.

John Barnes first caught the eye at international level with a spectacular solo goal against Brazil at the Maracana Stadium in Rio in 1984. He also impressed at the 1986 World Cup and was part of England's Italia 1990 campaign. The skilful winger was quick, strong on the ball and an excellent dribbler. A legend at Liverpool, Barnes scored spectacular goals and created countless chances for team-mates at all his clubs and for the Three Lions.

Tournaments & Rivals

England are one of the world's most successful football sides. This section covers all the major tournaments England have entered, as well as taking an in-depth look at their six greatest football rivals.

World Cup

England are one of just seven countries to have won the World Cup. They didn't enter the first three competitions, but when the 1950 tournament came around in Brazil, England were raring to go.

At the time, they were considered to be the best side in the world. Then came one of the biggest ever shocks in World Cup history – England lost 1-0 to the USA. Nowadays that would be like losing to a footballing minnow like San Marino or Andorra! They also lost their next game 1-0 to Spain and were soon packing their bags.

The 1954 Finals were held in Switzerland, and once again England sailed through the qualifying group, which was made up of the other home nations, Scotland, Wales and Northern Ireland. They reached the quarter-finals in the end before going out to Uruguay 4-2.

In 1958, the World Cup was staged in Sweden and this was to be the tournament when Brazil first showed their flair and brilliance. As for England, they had a side weakened by the loss of several players in the tragic Munich air crash, and limped out in the group stages.

Chile, in South America, was the venue for the 1962 competition. England arrived full of hope and played well to beat Argentina and qualify for the quarter-finals. They then met Brazil, and although they played well, finally lost out 3-1 to the eventual cup winners.

England captain Bobby Moore kissing the World Cup in 1966.

In 1966 the World Cup came to England and that summer there was a fantastic festival of football across the whole country. England made it through to a quarter-final with Argentina, which they won 1-0, before taking on Portugal in the semi-final. It turned out to be one of the best games of the tournament. England were two up before the famous Portuguese player Eusebio pulled one back with a penalty. The last eight minutes were frantic but England held on.

Expectations were high in Mexico for the 1970 tournament. After all, England were defending champions. England were drawn in the same group as Brazil but managed to scrape through and then took on their great rivals West Germany

in a quarter-final. But despite leading 2-0 they let the lead slip and went out 3-2 in extra time. Then came a very bleak 12 years as England failed to qualify for the finals in 1974 and 1978. England had some great players at the time such as Kevin Keegan, Tony Currie and Alan Hudson, but they couldn't seem to gel together as a team.

England returned to the world stage in Spain in 1982, but although they never lost a game – and only conceded one goal – their failure to score cost them dearly. They went out at the second round stage, just before the semi-finals.

79

World Cup

England were also goal shy at the 1986 Finals in Mexico. And they risked early elimination again until Gary Lineker's hat-trick against Poland. He scored two more against Paraguay to see England through to the quarters, where they came up against a Maradona-inspired Argentina, and went out 2-1.

At Italia 90 England did far better than anyone expected. Coming through a tricky group, they saw off Belgium in the second round and Cameroon in the quarters before going out to West Germany on penalties in the semi-final. They finally finished fourth, losing a third place play-off game with hosts Italy 2-1.

In 1994 there was more disappointment when England missed out on taking part in the first World Cup to be held in the USA.

In 1998 they crossed the English Channel to France, and again it was penalties that ended their hopes. Having scraped through to the second round they came up against Argentina and despite leading 2-1, they were eliminated after another dreaded shoot-out.

The England team wait anxiously for the penalty shoot-out.

ENGLAND

The 2002 Finals were the first to be held in Asia, with South Korea and Japan the joint hosts. Again, England made it through the opening rounds but this time came up against the mighty Brazil in the quarters, losing 2-1.

The last World Cup, in 2006, was held in Germany, but England never really got going. They eased through their group but once again went out on penalties, this time to Portugal.

And so to 2010, when the World Cup will be hosted by South Africa for the first time. Let's see what happens!

Beckham, Owen and Danny Mills celebrate after scoring against Brazil in the 2002 World Cup.

For the Record
England at the World Cup

Year	England	Winners
1930	did not enter	Winners: Uruguay
1934	did not enter	Winners: Italy
1938	did not enter	Winners: Italy
1950	out at group stage	Winners: Uruguay
1954	quarter-finals	Winners: West Germany
1958	out at group stage	Winners: Brazil
1962	quarter-finals	Winners: Brazil
1966	winners	
1970	quarter-finals	Winners: Brazil
1974	did not qualify	Winners: West Germany
1978	did not qualify	Winners: Argentina
1982	second round	Winners: Italy
1986	quarter-finals	Winners: Argentina
1990	fourth	Winners: West Germany
1994	did not qualify	Winners: Brazil
1998	second round	Winners: France
2002	quarter-finals	Winners: Brazil
2006	quarter-finals	Winners: Italy

ENGLAND

European Championship

England standing together as a team.

England have always performed pretty well in the World Cup but they haven't yet lived up to their potential in the European Championship. Played every four years, the goal is to find the best footballing country in Europe.

England opted out of the first tournament and perhaps wished they'd given the second competition a wide berth, too, with France knocking them out 6-3 over two matches in 1963.

In 1968 they got through to the semi-finals, before losing to Yugoslavia. However they did beat the Soviet Union in a play-off for third place,

which was to prove their best ever finish. England cruised through qualifying in 1972, dropping just one point. But they came up against West Germany in the quarter-final. Having lost 3-1 at Wembley, the 0-0 draw in Berlin was no use to them, and they were out. In 1976 they failed to qualify but were unbeaten in the run up to the 1980 Finals, which were held in just one country, Italy, for the first time. But England flopped and didn't make it through the group stage.

They missed out again in 1984, finishing second in their qualifying group to Denmark, but their tails were up again in 1988 after they edged into the finals in West Germany.

European Championship

ENGLAND

But then it all went wrong. They finished bottom of their group, with just one point and two goals from three games.

In 1996 England hosted the tournament and the team played some of their best football since the 1966 World Cup. Alan Shearer was scoring goals for fun and Paul Gascoigne was in excellent form. Scotland and Spain were beaten along the way to a semi-final encounter with Germany, where England lost a nail-biting penalty shoot-out.

In 2000, despite a great start – England were two up against Portugal after just 18 minutes in their opening game – and were out in the first round. And it was Portugal that did it to England again in 2004, beating them on penalties in the thrilling quarter-finals (see page 62).

In 2008 Austria and Switzerland will share the finals and England, who failed to qualify, still won't be able to put an end to their European Championship jinx.

Alan Shearer celebrates victory!

For the Record
England in the European Championship

1960 – did not enter	Winners: Soviet Union (Russia)
1964 – out in first round	Winners: Spain
1968 – third	Winners: Italy
1972 – quarter-finals	Winners: West Germany
1976 – did not qualify	Winners: Czechoslovakia
1980 – out at group stage	Winners: West Germany
1984 – did not qualify	Winners: France
1988 – out at group stage	Winners: Holland
1992 – out at group stage	Winners: Denmark
1996 – semi-finals	Winners: Germany
2000 – out at group stage	Winners: France
2004 – quarter-finals	Winners: Greece

Rivals
Germany

From World Cup Finals to nail-biting penalty shoot-outs, there's no getting away from it – England and Germany are the greatest rivals in world football. (Just for the record, Germany was known as West Germany between 1954-1990.) It all began with a 3-3 draw in May 1930 but it wasn't until England won the 1966 World Cup Final 4-2 (see page 55) that the rivalry really started to heat up.

Germany took their revenge four years later in the heat of Mexico, sending England crashing out of the World Cup at the quarter-final stage, 3-2. Incredibly, England had been 2-0 up as well.

Many people say it took England well over ten years to recover from the shock! What is true is that they failed to even qualify for the next two finals.

There was more English pain two years later when Germany won 3-1 at Wembley to dump England out of the European Championship. A 0-0 draw in the 1982 World Cup helped to eliminate England from yet another competition, so the players who lined up to face Germany in the semi-final of Italia 1990 can be forgiven for being a little bit worried!

Graeme Le Saux avoids being tackled by a German defender.

ENGLAND

England fell behind on the hour mark but equalised through Gary Lineker with ten minutes to go. There were no more goals, so the game went to extra time. But still the deadlock wasn't broken so the game went to penalties. With England 4-3 down, Chris Waddle had to score England's fourth kick. Unfortunately, so the joke goes, the ball is still orbiting the moon today! Poor Chris blazed it miles over the bar and England were knocked out by the Germans yet again.

In 1996 they met again, this time in the semi-final of the European Championship (see page 59). But once again, England's penalty jinx struck. Alan Shearer scored the only goal in a 1-0 win in a group game at Euro 2000 and then came two qualifying games for the 2002 World Cup.

The first saw Germany win 1-0 in the last ever international game at the old Wembley. It also proved to be Kevin Keegan's last game in charge. But then came Munich 2001, which is a match no England fan will ever forget. And so the rivalry goes on and England just about have the upper hand at the moment – as long as the game doesn't go to penalties that is!

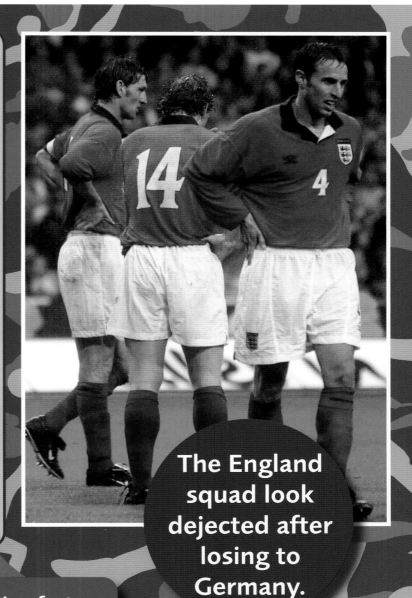

The England squad look dejected after losing to Germany.

For the Record

England v Germany

Played	26
Won	11
Drawn	5
Lost	10
Goals for	45
Goals against	33

Amazing fact:
England played East Germany four times in friendlies, winning three and drawing once.

Rivals
France

There's always been a healthy rivalry between England and France, whether at football, rugby, or even tiddlywinks! To start with, the football matches were one-sided affairs and it was England, not France, who were magnifique! England won 11 of the first 12 games, including a 6-0 win in France and a 3-0 win at Arsenal's old Highbury Ground in 1947.

The first major clash came in the European Nations Cup (now known as the European Championship). After a 1-1 draw at Wembley, England went to Paris but were soundly thrashed 5-2.

They met again during the 1966 World Cup and this time it was England's turn to celebrate, with a 2-0 win.

The teams avoided each other throughout the 1970s but met again during the 1982 World Cup in Spain. And what a welcome England gave France, with Bryan Robson scoring after just 27 seconds! England finally won 3-1, which was no mean achievement against a French team that would go on to become one of the best teams in the world.

There's not much to say about the bore draw at the 1992 European Championship in Sweden, so we'll move on to the most recent match between the two sides. It's one that most England fans will want to forget!

Lampard and Gerrard celebrate scoring against France.

ENGLAND

Portugal 2004 and England faced France, the defending European Champions. Frank Lampard had headed England into the lead after 38 minutes and, although David Beckham later missed a penalty, England were holding on. And as the 90 minutes were up, they looked set for a famous victory.

But they hadn't reckoned on Zinedine Zidane. First he curled a free-kick past David James in the England goal to make it 1-1. Then, in what was the last attack of the match, James fouled Thierry Henry in the box – penalty.

Cool as you like, up stepped Zidane again, calmly slotting the ball home and giving France an unbelievable extra-time victory.

For the Record
England v France

Played	26
Won	16
Drawn	4
Lost	6
Goals for	65
Goals against	32

Sol Campbell controlling the ball against France.

Amazing fact:

Masek scored after 15 seconds in Czechoslovakia v Mexico in 1962. This was the quickest goal in World Cup history until Hakan Sukur scored after just 11 seconds for Turkey in 2002.

Rivals
Brazil

England's games against the mighty Brazil have actually been few and far between. But when the Three Lions do come up against the Boys from Brazil, there's never a dull moment! The first big encounter came during the 1958 World Cup Finals in Sweden when they played out the first 0-0 draw in World Cup history.

They met again four years later in the quarter-finals of the 1962 World Cup when Brazil were convincing 3-1 winners. The match is best remembered for a dog running on the pitch and the England striker Jimmy Greaves going down on all fours to try and encourage it to leave! In 1970 they were drawn in the same group during the Mexico World Cup. And this time the memorable moment was an incredible save by the great English keeper Gordon Banks.

Pele, probably the most famous footballer ever, sent a powerful header towards goal. And he was already starting to celebrate his 'goal' when, in a flash, Banks dived to his right and just managed to tip the ball over the bar. Although England played well, they finally lost 1-0.

A dozen friendlies followed until the sides met at the quarter-final stage again, this time in Japan at the 2002 World Cup. And it turned out to be another cracker! England scored first, with Michael Owen's pace opening up the Brazilian defence, before he confidently chipped the ball over the keeper. But Brazil equalised on the stroke of half-time.

Gary Lineker, trying to beat Brazil's defence.

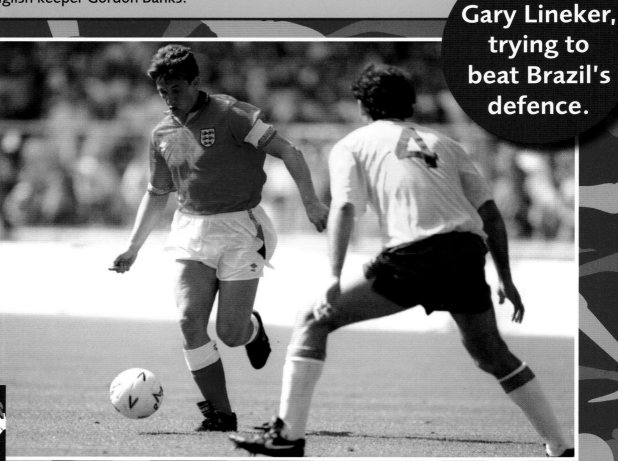

Then, after just five minutes of the second half, Ronaldinho sent a high, hopeful free-kick into the box. But it caught England keeper David Seaman off guard. He back-pedalled furiously but couldn't stop it dropping in under the bar at the far post.

But the twists kept on coming and just eight minutes later the goalscorer was harshly sent off, forcing Brazil to play out the final half an hour with just ten men. But try as they might, England couldn't get back on level terms.

In all, England have only beaten Brazil three times. But there's always an intense rivalry between the countries. After all, England 'invented' the modern game, while the Brazilians have shown us all how to play it!

For the Record
England v Brazil

Played	22
Won	3
Drawn	9
Lost	10
Goals for	19
Goals against	30

Amazing fact:

A team has only scored more than two goals in four of the 22 games between the two countries.

Michael Owen celebrates scoring against Brazil in 2000.

Over 90 minutes at least, England have a very good record against Argentina. But over the years there are two games in particular that stand out – unfortunately England lost them both! After a couple of friendlies, the first competitive meeting came in 1962, when England ran out 3-1 winners in a World Cup group game.

Then came a momentous clash in the quarter-final of the 1966 World Cup. The Argentina skipper Antonio Rattin became the first ever player to be sent off in an England home game. The South Americans never really recovered, with England winning 1-0 in the end.

But it was to be another World Cup quarter-final twenty years later, this time at the Azteca Stadium in Mexico City, where the rivalry hit boiling point. 'Hand ball!' protested the England players. 'Goal,' said the referee. Maradona went wild, although he would later describe it as the 'Hand of God' goal – in other words admitting he had punched the ball in.

England had done well to get this far, while Argentina were coasting thanks largely to one man, a footballing genius by the name of Diego Maradona. The first half was goalless and England were holding their own. Then Maradona challenged the England keeper Peter Shilton for a high ball in the box. And suddenly the ball was in the net.

For the Record

England v Argentina

Played	13
Won	6
Drawn	5
Lost	2
Goals for	21
Goals against	15

Beckham being shown a red card in a 1998 game.

But minutes later, the other Maradona appeared – Maradona the magician, as he dribbled his way past half the England team to slot the ball home. Gary Lineker scored late on but England were out.

Fast forward 12 years to France and a World Cup second round clash. This time Argentina took the lead, scoring a penalty in the first few minutes. But England were soon level with a goal of their own – Alan Shearer scored from the penalty spot.

Cue Michael Owen. Picking the ball up on the halfway line he ran and ran and ran before unleashing a shot that flew past the keeper. But by half-time Argentina had equalised once more. Then disaster struck. Just two minutes into the second period and David Beckham was sent off. England held on for penalties, but their record in shoot-outs was woeful. And sadly nothing changed that night as they lost 4-3 on penalties. But revenge, so the saying goes, is sweet and the two sides met once more in a group match at Japan's Sapporo Dome at the 2002 World Cup. And this time they did score a penalty, Beckham coverting to see England home 1-0.

Even the last time they met, in a friendly in 2005, proved to be eventful. With just three minutes left, Argentina looked to be home and dry at 2-1 up. But they hadn't reckoned on Michael Owen again, who popped up with two late goals to seal a remarkable 3-2 win.

Michael Owen tackling Argentinian Juan Veron.

Amazing fact:

The second time the two teams met, in May 1953, goes down in history as only one of the two times an England game has ever been abandoned. The reason – torrential Argentine rain.

Team Profile

The England v Austria line-up for their game in 2007.

Front row, left to right:

Michael Owen, Wayne Bridge, Joe Cole and Steven Gerrard

Team Profile

ENGLAND

Back row, left to right:

David Beckham, Scott Carson, Peter Crouch, Micah Richards, Joleon Lescott, Sol Campbell and Frank Lampard

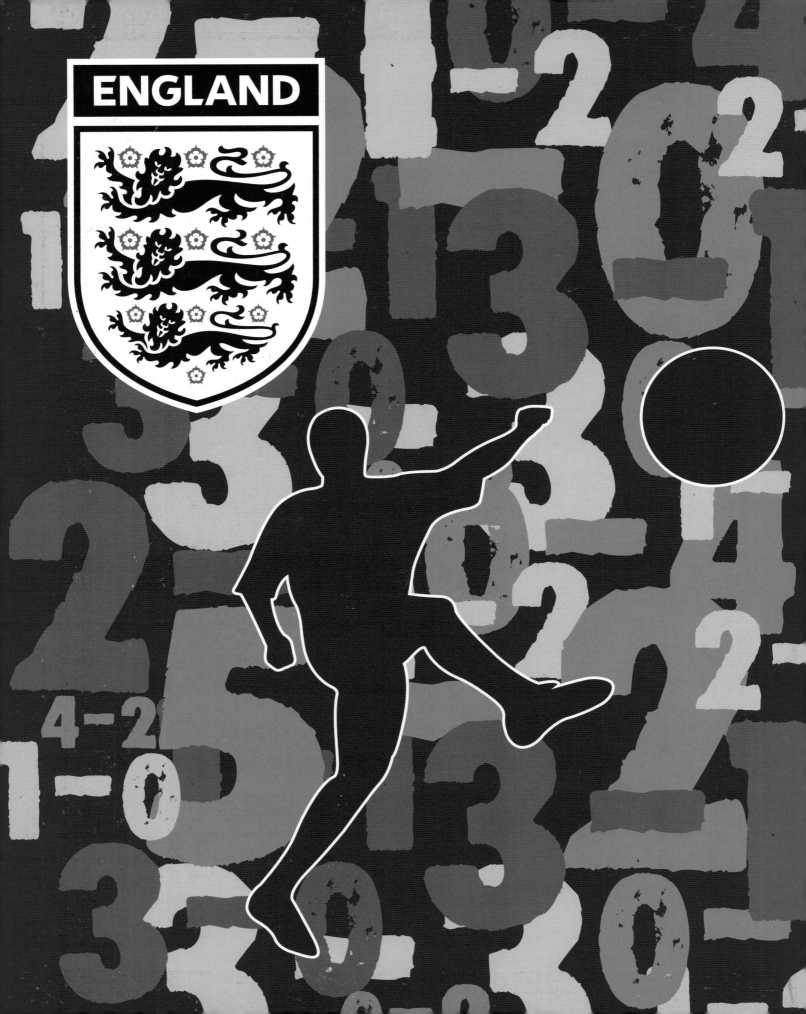